# THE LITTLE RED BOOK OF BIG SOULFUL LOVE

COURAGEOUS

To all the lovers you'll meet in these pages.
Their contributions have been priceless and intimate.
They gave from their heart and revealed vulnerability.
A few bravely told about their pain of not feeling loved and not being able to give their love.

The Little Red Book of Big Soulful Love



Extraordinary Measures Publishing

ISBN 979-8-9954845-0-9



Printed in the United States of America

# Contents

Alex was my "dream helper" and turned my raw drawing into the real vision.

**Alex was the agent for my first book. He did such a masterful job it was a success, so I wanted him to be my agent again for this book. He currently teaches at a Texas University; he has been involved for several decades in the Institute of Endocentric Psychology from Mexico. His brilliance and creativity are exceptional.**

**Alex can grasp the vision I have in my mind and transform it into a masterpiece and hits my target. He's the son of my treasured friends Marco and Lupita Nunez. He's the powerhouse behind the success of this book on love.**

# THE POWER OF LOVE AND POSITIVITY

*(Author: Steve)*

Note from Sidney,
When I worked for Steve, his leadership style and positivity intrigued me. Steve came to this work location a month before he could bring his wife and children. He made a statement that stuck with me for over 30 years, as did his radiant positivity. He said, "If you think I am on fire with energy now, Sidney, wait till Donna joins me. I will be a bonfire of flames!"

My hometown was Dayton, Ohio. Donna and I went to the same high school for four years. We were friends but had never dated. I went off to college. When I came back for spring break, my intuition was pushing me to go by her house and say hello.

Donna sparkled with a bubbly personality, yet she was down-to-earth and a well-grounded young lady. I was excited by her energy and felt a soothing stability. She was so positive, and that matched me. It felt right being with her.

Our first date was going to a nearby park to get acquainted, and 56 days later we were married.

**I knew I wanted to be with her kind of energy and acceptance. It was as if I had waited for Donna all my life.**

**She searches for ways to help our families, even nephews and nieces. One day she was really sick, and I told her to stay home to rest. She said, "I can't, it's Swam's birthday and she is counting on both of us to be there." Our niece Swam's name means golden child.**

**My favorite philosophy is to do what you do with a positive heart; otherwise, why bother? I love Donna's caring heart. Throughout our marriage, she has never deviated from her joyful nature. She fulfilled my needs. I always felt her admiration.**

**When I grappled with cancer, Donna was right there by my side, supporting me in all possible ways. I can count on her to be my positive-thinking partner, doing what is required without holding back. With her care and belief in me, I knew I could conquer any battle, and that helped me do just that: win the battle.**

**When we had struggles, they were dwarfed by the overwhelming power of our love. Forgiveness was quick and easy for us.**

**It is my privilege to take care of Donna now that she needs it. We are a team, partners for life. We feel blessed in our union and never take it for granted. Rather, it is to be celebrated.**

**The strength of our dedication and love got us through the good times and the horror of losing our twin girls. Yvonne and Yvette died a short time from each other in their late twenties. The loss of a child is like no other pain; it cannot be cured. Donna and I held on**

**tight to each other. Our hearts stood still with grief, but there was no such thing as quitting. We kept affirming each other until we re-found our safe haven and could breathe once more.**

**The last message I want Donna to hear from me is, "Donna, I love you with all my heart. THANK YOU FOR LOVING ME WITH ALL YOUR HEART."**

Donna and Steve still grinning with mischief after all these years.

# SHORT SHORTS SET THE NIGHT ON FIRE

*(Author: Donna)*

**Steve and I went to the same high school for four years. He didn't talk to me and we did not date. However, I did notice how handsome he was. His smile was luscious and twinkled like stars in the night sky. He seemed to have been born with a fetching smile etched on his face.**

**Steve's positive attitude radiated warmth and an invitation. I was smitten, no doubt about it. Someone had to strike the match that would ignite our flame within. It might as well be me.**

**He left for college and I engaged in summer activities with my girlfriends, basking in the sun while a burning flame was melting my heart.**

**One day Steve showed up again from his college break. I went into my room and put on short shorts and a halter top. Mom gave me the raised-eyebrow look. I said, "I just want Steve to notice me." He was so fine in every way. Well, he did notice me alright and came back like a firefly searching for its mate.**

**I swooned. He came back the next day, and sparks crackled in the air. We were seeing each other often. It felt so good because he saw the positive side of**

everything. We matched. Our relationship felt natural and right. We were harmonious and compatible. I thrilled at his touch.

Steve told me he had to get ready to go back to college, and he wanted to see me when he finished school. I said, "Why don't we just go ahead and get married. Why wait?" He smiled and said, "Well, okay."

We went to a high-class wedding at the Justice of the Peace in Dayton and got married. Our wedding dinner was a cheeseburger and chocolate milk at Burger King. We were ecstatic and having fun. The best was yet to come. We headed for Cleveland for our honeymoon. We had a nice room at the Holiday Inn. Steve took us out for a proper dinner. And it was crazy romantic. My heart twittered. I was one lucky girl.

Our life was on a trajectory to just grow and grow. We delighted in the life we created. Love is a big word in our relationship. We had twin girls, Yvonne and Yvette. We marveled at the joy they gave us and the fun it was raising them. Our happiness overflowed.

I ABANDONED ALL FEAR AND GAVE MY HEART TOTALLY TO YOU STEVE.

# BULLIES BEWARE

*(Author: Cindy)*

I love Darrell because he is a nurturer, he is dependable, and loyal to the bone.

He is respectful and he is my best friend. Our conversation is reassuring because no topic is off limits. We create a safe place.

I feel loved when he is concerned about my health. I don't stand up for myself, so I feel sheltered and protected when Darrell won't let anyone bully me or disrespect me.

He always kisses me goodnight and it is such a loving feeling. Darrell knows how to calm me down when I feel excited and go off the deep end. When a panic attack attempts to disable me, he gets me in the car, drives me around, and talks soothingly to me until the panic dries up.

When I'm not reasonable he gives me reasonable thoughts, so I don't spin out of control. This builds my confidence.

He always praises my creativity, and I love the way this builds me up.

I want to give Darrell the reassurance that I will not run away from him; I also need to give him the stability to not spend beyond our means.

**I want to give him a more orderly home, because that is important to him. What is important to Darrell is important to me. We are one.**

**Darrell, I admire and cherish you. You have been my backbone and shield. You are my refuge. I bask in the safety of your arms. YOU EMBRACE ME WITH YOUR FIERCE PROTECTION.**

In love in Italy, still in love.

# MY FOREVER PLEDGE OF LOVE

*(Author: Darrell)*

I view love as a deep understanding of my mate.

To be able to see all sides of her, the good parts and the bad parts, no matter what, and I accept her for who and what she is.

I will support Cindy through all times. Her strength and energy excite me, and I find it very lovable.

For me to feel loved, I need commitment and presence.

I want Cindy to desire to be with me. I want her to feel my love and accept me in her heart. I support her and pledge to be there for her. She can count on me. I MAY BE SHORT BUT IN MY MIND I AM 6 FEET TALL, I WILL PROTECT CINDY.

Being together is a chance to love. Being in bed together, watching TV together, it all fills my cup.

If I could make one request, it would be for Cindy to curb spending too much money because it causes me stress.

I will never leave her. I will love Cindy forever.

Cindy I love you and everything will work out OK. Our marriage has been more than I could have ever dreamed of. We did more in one day than most couples do in a month.

IT HAS BEEN ONE HECK OF A RIDE!

# CUPID'S ARROW MISSED THE MARK

*(Author: Patricia)*

**Though I have not had the opportunity to experience the kind of love I yearn for, I do know what it is, what I ache for.**

**My first marriage was to an alcoholic and unfaithful man, so we eventually divorced. I felt abandoned, betrayed, and used.**

**I was so raw and vulnerable, I lived only for our children. There was a lot of pain. Seeing them exposed to his uncontrollable drinking caused all of us a lot of pain. I remained alone for a long time, seeking help for my own healing.**

**My second husband was a long-term business associate. One day he asked me if we could take our friendship to the next level. We dated for 2 years and married. At last, I felt like I had found happiness. However, 18 months into our marriage, he was diagnosed with prefrontal lobe dementia. I experienced the painful loss of connection, one agonizing day after another. He slipped and faded away until one day he no longer understood I was his wife. I was just a nice woman who took care of him, but his dull eyes could no longer witness me as significant.**

With him, I felt an emptiness that hurt deep inside me. What would my future hold? I no longer had a helpmate but had the responsibility to care for my new husband. I was already sharing the care with my sister for our mentally challenged brother.

On top of all of these pressures, I had the daily task of trying to encourage my basement-bound daughter. I want her to get a job or go to school and make a life for herself. I am taking care of a man that I don't get to have as a husband. I feel too burdened and overwhelmed to allow the sunlight of joy to lift my heart.

However, I do know what I yearn for.

I yearn for love that is other-centered in both of us. There would be respect and authenticity of interest in each other at the soul level of caring. We would actually want to be mature in our connection until we could know each other at the soul depth and help each other heal from our past wounds.

There would be generosity of caring and love. To not be stingy with those actions that can heal and comfort. We would be quick to forgive, be patient, and be peacemakers for each other.

Trust is crucial to resolve issues for our equal contentment.

I would want for me and a mate to develop a deep, true love. One that has unquestionable loyalty and transparency no matter what. On this we could build love that is absolutely SAFE emotionally.

Love requires a willingness to sacrifice for each other and be equally committed to each other's good.

Fearless openness hides no secrets.

**LOVE IS TO BE A SAFE HAVEN OF PEACE. THIS IS WHAT MY HEART YEARNS FOR!**

Patricia's radiance prevails.

# EAT PRAY LOVE

*(Author: Bo)*

What I love and appreciate about my wife Janet is how intelligent she is and a great mother to our son.

She cooks very healthy and nourishing meals. It makes me feel cared for and loved. We happily work together to keep our surroundings orderly and clean.

When we have to be apart, Janet puts together meals, so I won't die. It gives me the feeling of being valued.

She goes on outdoor adventures with me, and we really enjoy the exploration.

I want to give her companionship and a lovely home. It pleases me with my skill in carpentry that I can create the dreams she has for our home.

We are a team in decorating our new home and have a common eye for beauty. It's a comfort and we really enjoy the results that we achieve together.

One thing that I want is more understanding from her. I want her to know who I really am.

If she asked me for anything, I'd do my best to give it to her as long as it was reasonable. It pleases me to do things that make Janet feel loved. For instance, I built her a garden shed, remodeled our home to her liking, and am engaged in planning an outdoor kitchen for our new Arizona home.

**We are committed to each other for a lifetime, so we can always give our son a solid foundation.**
**OUR LIVING STYLE AT THIS POINT IS LOVING, WARM, ACCEPTING, AND FULLFILLING.**

Bo and Janet in the lap of love and joy. He calls her, “my peanut”.

# BE MY LIFE'S COMPANION AND WE'LL NEVER GROW OLD

*(Author: Janet)*

What I love about Jerry is his great sense of humor. He knows how to turn everyday incidents into fun and laughter. Jerry is passionate about life. He is kind and adores little children. I haven't seen a child yet being able to resist his loving attention. He can be very thoughtful.

When he does things for me, or says kind and loving words to me, or shows his tender affection, I feel cherished.

In turn, I like to give him the acceptance he deserves and needs. It is fun to explore with him our common sense of humor about the creeks and grunts of aging.

Being a good companion is a shared value. We both believe in God and share our spiritual values.

Just having togetherness is love. We love to go exploring together. We went to get a mutual massage, and the sensual pleasure was swoon-worthy. We felt so connected. We love sunshine.

We both struggle with the deprivation of sunlight in gray Michigan, so we built our home near Sedona, Arizona, to be drenched in sunshine.

JERRY IS MY LIFE'S COMPANION.

# BETRAYAL BEYOND THE GRAVE

*(Author: Lynda)*

I look at love as an action that takes place. You can see it, hear it and feel it. My husband did simple acts because it gave me pleasure.

He was very limited physically. After a hard day at work, I could come home, lie on the sofa, knowing he would rub my tired feet. It's not that he wanted to, but he did it because he knew I loved it.

We dated 2 years and were married 6 years.

I learned the sad truth and risk in a relationship. The closer you allow yourself to be to another, the greater the danger is for more hurt.

He died in 2020. One day I was missing him badly, so I scrolled through his cell phone. To my shock I discovered he had been having an affair. He was unfaithful.

My trust was shattered and my heart cracked and broke in my chest. I was humiliated to the core. I plunged headlong into dark, ominous depression. I was stripped of any way to protect myself. I sank into, and was consumed, by my own misery.

I made excuses to avoid God's comfort and had to force myself to go to church occasionally.

I found a grief group and went through their course to work out my anger, but I was still only half living.

Planning a vacation with my friend helped take my mind off myself for a while. I started seeing a therapist and a glimmer of hope sneaked in. Volunteering to be a grief group leader helped me dissolve most of my anger. Now I can focus on the good, yet feelings of SAFETY eluded me.

Now I choose to let go of the anguish of betrayal because it is toxic to my soul. I had a choice to hang onto the bad stuff, or I could kiss it goodbye, so I kissed it.

I want to be like a Sidney or a Paula who live with bright enthusiasm even when they endure hard circumstances. I want to live with Joy, to have Hope and inhale it into my body and exhale brightness of the shining stars.

I wish I could have given John peace. The accident he was in killed his Dad and he felt GUILTY and responsible for his Dad's death. He needed peace and acceptance and probably forgiveness.

I doubt myself, so I strive for hope in my future. I intend to get better every day. It would be nice to have a companion, but I don't think I could put myself in that vulnerable position again.

I HAVE A GOOD LIFE! That is what I remind myself of every day. I do mourn that I didn't get to experience true relational love and the loyalty I craved.

GOD GOT ME THIS FAR, I TRUST HE WILL TAKE ME TO THE END.

I am determined to find hope and joy in my life.

# FEARLESS LOVE

*(Author: Dennis)*

I believe love is being best friends and being attracted to each other. Love is a many-faceted thing that causes us to be balanced.

Rochelle and I are always together. There is no single-sided attraction. We love each other physically, mentally, and spiritually.

We have common interests yet appreciate our differences. We appreciate each other for who we are and do not try to change each other.

Rochelle listens and cares about my outcomes. She genuinely tries to help my desired outcomes become a reality for me.

I trust her. She is my confidant. I want to put her first.

She is selfless and understands the commitment we have to each other. We gladly endure all things. I love that we share our love for God and acts of service for our church family.

When we are apart, I miss her company. Being able to be close is something I value.

It conquers that lonely separation feeling. When we are together, I get to have her whole person.

We do fun things together. The fun things we've done, like visiting Disney World several times makes us happy. Being happy together gives us that sense of wholeness.

My parents had a wonderful, loving marriage, and that gave me a pattern on which to build my own relationship. Their love had a big impact on me, which gave me courage and the ability to give my love fearlessly with no holdbacks.

I want Rochelle to understand that what I need from her is to feel loved by her friendship.

You can't turn your back on your best friend, so I make Rochelle my best friend.

It has been a delight and privilege to raise our children together. Our children have added great joy to our lives.

I realize that love is a mystery and that intrigues me.

Love is a feeling so special and unique that it can only be understood by experiencing it.

Love will take us to the mountaintop. It also needs to be with us in the valleys as well.

I will cry with Rochelle and I will mourn with her when she needs it. This will give us both the strength to continue on.

Marriage and love are not a 50%/50% deal. Marriage and love are 100%/100%. It requires us both to give our all to each other. We need to want to bring happiness to our mate.

Love creates an unbreakable bond.

I AM ECSTATIC, MARRIED TO ROCHELLE. MY HEART IS AT PEACE.

# THE DELIGHTFUL LAUGH GOT ME

*(Author: Alan)*

Ann and I have been bound in marriage for 24 short years. What a serendipitous beginning.

I was won over by Ann's infectious laugh. It was like little crystal bells delicately ringing in my ears. So mystical, I had to laugh with her.

There are so many traits I love about Ann. She is a great Mother. She does wife so well she should win a prize.

We run towards joy together, like kids who are thrilled to run to a playground.

I want to give Ann the depth of my love at the soul level and support her tenaciously.

Ann praises me when I am doing things well. When I mess up, she kindly but firmly lets me know. Then we are once again balanced.

It is important that Ann hears me say, "Thank you for sharing your life with me, but I am not going anywhere. We are bound together with Gorilla Glue. And you know what that means. IT MEANS WE ARE INSEPARABLE."

Ann's feminine sensuality was an irresistible perfume to Alan's heart.

The beginning of a wedded bliss

# THE GLINT IN YOUR EYES

*(Author: Ann)*

Alan and I met on a blind date in Ann Arbor and what a glorious start it was.

I was drawn to Alan's quirky sense of humor.

I appreciated his confidence; it made him more appealing to me.

A real positive for me was the discovery HE DID NOT BITE HIS NAILS. That could have been a real deal breaker.

What cements my love for him is that Alan makes me feel heard. I mean at the center of my heart, he really hears me.

I can trust Alan and count on him when I need him. Because of his love for me I am never alone in this life. This action sends me the message that I am secure and protected by him.

He is an amazing husband and father.

I will give Alan a lifetime of continuous love, respect, and support. I desire the same from him.

Alan hears me when I say, "Thank you for asking me to marry you. I ALWAYS WANT TO SEE THE SHINY GLINT OF LOVE DANCE IN YOUR EYES."

# BE THE BEST YOU CAN BE

*(Author: Mike)*

My wife Cathy is very decisive. There are no gray areas, and I love that about her.

She is loving and will do anything to please me. I just want to be sure she also pleases herself.

She is upbeat most of the time, and I love to see and experience her joyfulness.

Her nature is to be outgoing and friendly, and this helps draw me out of my shell.

Cathy takes excellent care of herself. She goes to the gym and keeps a luscious body, but she also shines with a refreshing physical beauty. She wants to be the best she can be.

All these actions make me feel loved. I want to give her understanding of who I am so she can accept both the best of me and the human side of me.

I am more in love with Cathy today than when we first fell in love. There is a lot of infatuation in new love. I love her way beyond that. She has a depth that emerges with the passage of time.

We have common interests of physical fitness, eating healthy food, caring for our longevity, dancing, and spiritual love of God.

Cathy and I are inseparable. I prefer her company over my buddies. I am proud of her.

**I feel emotionally safe with her. When we have to be apart, I miss our companionship.**

**We recently got a beautiful little dog, Lucy, and it is so joyful for both of us. We wish we would have gotten her sooner because we get to pour our love into the same thing.**

**CATHY IS MY FOREVER SWEETHEART.**

(Lucy the dog) "I love Lucy I love Cathy", "I love Lucy I love Mike" and the winner with the most votes is: LUCY!

# TOGETHER FOREVER

*(Author: Cathy)*

Love to me is respect, admiration and selflessness.

Love is when we work together on little and big personal projects and accomplish a pleasing outcome. We both want to have harmony in all our results.

Love is being aware and willingly doing tasks without having to be asked.

I want to be supported and lifted up by Mike. He is my "Rock". This makes me feel protected and secure. I know he will stand between me and any threat of harm.

I want to give Mike support, affirmation, and compassion.

We have a valued friendship. I would do anything to make him happy.

Mike is an outstanding provider. That makes me feel important, secure and cherished. I admire his desire to do this for me because it is healing old wounds.

Mike is quiet, so I would like to have more conversation. But I do know he has the absolute desire to take care of me.

We tenaciously stick together through the good times and the hard times, and cling to living out our vows no matter what.

WE DANCE JOYFULLY THROUGH OUR AMAZING LIFE TOGETHER!

# PASSIONATE LOVE

*(Author: Marco)*

For me, love is a desire to serve, where I am willing to give my all to my mate. Lupita is the only love of my life. I have just a few friends and she fulfilled that need in my soul. She became and is my friend.

Our passion transformed into understanding and respect for each other.

Lupita offers me her love by creating an oasis of love. We have moved so many times, and she always changes a house into a beautiful and warm home no matter where we are.

What I need from her is to see her and to feel her touch. I crave attention and physical affection. So, when she gives it to me I feel her love.

I went through a spiritually broken crisis, and it nearly destroyed us. But we hung on to our commitment and love to each other.

When I went through a period of deep depression because of family betrayal I didn't want to do anything, I didn't want to go to work, I was empty. Lupita said, "I can't stand to see you this way, you have so much to offer, so you must do something or our family will starve." She pushed me out of depression into lifesaving action.

**When I received certification for my new business of spinal readjustments I wondered how to market it. Lupita immediately had flyers made and went all around the area encouraging people to come to my clinic. I was amazed at her level of support and boldness. I rediscovered my sense of purpose.**

**I thank God she always believed in me.**

**WE WILL PUT OUR FEARS ASIDE AND REAFFIRM OUR GLORIOUS LOVE.**

The most beautiful flower in town and the Caballero who scooped her up and galloped into the flaming sun.

# ROBUST LAUGHTER IS MUSIC TO MY EARS

*(Author: Lupita)*

Love is giving. I love to give delicious food and time to Marco. I feel warm in his presence, and I want to make him feel that same way. I believe that the kitchen is the heart and soul of our home. I am most comfortable when I can give from my kitchen. To me this is giving my love.

I feel cared for if he cheerfully does something I need done. That makes me feel important to him.

I want to feel Marco's strength when I ask for his help and he gives it cheerfully.

I feel loved when we are together, holding hands, and being aware of each other.

I want to give Marco affection and more loving communication.

It fulfills me to cook and make him the good food he loves.

It would thrill me to make him feel joyful, alive, and happy. I want to hear his robust laughter.

I want him to be with me, so I can feel secure because he is my protector.

I FEEL SAFE WHEN WE ARE TOGETHER HOLDING HANDS.

# TWO LIFETIMES OF BLESSED LOVE

*(Author: Anonymous)*

In my early years of marriage, my husband was the love of my life. After his death, I remained alone for several years.

My current husband is the love of my life at this latter part of my life.

How many people are blessed with such love twice in one lifetime? We have a low-keyed life of love.

LIVING IS EASY. IT IS COMFORTABLE AND SAFE.

# MY SAFE SANCTUARY

*(Author: Jane)*

In the beginning, I found Roger so fascinating and interesting. As time took us to a deeper connection, I got jitters in my stomach and couldn't wait to see him again.

As it matured into love, there was respect, commitment, and steadfastness. That turned into an unshakable trust.

Love is a choice to show up with love in my heart, even if I didn't feel like it that day. This commitment is important to me.

Roger gives me a hug every morning, and I get a hug every night. We don't leave each other without a hug, so every beginning and every ending, I get a hug and feel so special.

He is welcoming and accepting, and he touches me.

I feel like Roger is my sanctuary. He never criticizes me but only has good to say. He makes it clear he wants me just as I am. One time I mentioned I had gained some weight and he said, "You don't hear me complaining". He accepts and protects me. I want to give him these same soothing feelings.

I admire Roger as a man and want him to know I adore him. When we are apart, I miss the adventure he creates in my life. We laugh a lot, and I feel safe in the

**joy of our compatibility. Roger came in under the radar. There is a depth to him, and he is so interesting.**

**I CHERISH ALL ASPECTS ABOUT ROGER.**

There's a joyful lot of hugging going on in our relationship, we are definitely not hug deprived.

# JUST AS I AM

*(Author: Roger)*

When I examine my love for Jane, the first thing that comes to mind is respect for each other and for being on each other's side. This assures that we are not alone.

Loyalty is important to both of us.

Jane and I are in physical contact most of the time, holding hands and hugging. We are greatly compatible and enjoy the warmth of touch.

She calls me every day at 4:30 p.m. from the company she owns. Her consistency makes me feel loved and adored. It feels so good that she is thinking about me.

This keeps us on track with a consistency that helps me a lot.

We never criticize each other but accept each other as we are.

There are no secrets. We share openly, and it makes me feel emotionally safe with Jane.

Family is important to us, and we make it a point to be in our siblings' lives.

For Valentine's Day I made her a large valentine from paint, glitter and crystal. I did it to show her how special she is to me. It meant a lot to her because she herself is a creative artist.

**When we are apart, I look forward with great anticipation to being near her again.**

**I deeply love Jane and getting to share all that we have.**

**Jane calls me her sanctuary, when we embrace in a tender hug, she is also my sanctuary.**

**SHE IS MY SAFE PLACE.**

# FAMILY TRADITIONS AND HIS GENEROUS GIFTS OF LOVE

*(Author: Liz)*

Love for me has to include a physical connection. Brent and I believe in being kind to each other.

We complement each other.

Brent and I share our efforts, our plans, and help each other.

We share quality time and love physical affection.

I need patience and forgiveness to feel loved. I need to feel emotionally connected to Brent.

When he speaks words of affection to me, without distraction, I know he is accepting me. This understanding makes me feel adored.

He hears me and really focuses on what I'm saying. His deep acceptance makes me feel safe.

Brent is my soulmate. I am touched by his tender heart.

He is empathetic to me and others in hardships. I love this tender side of him.

Brent is an excellent father and puts much energy into keeping our family ties together. He promotes closeness among his siblings, our children, and grandchildren in our traditional outings.

**Brent told me I had given him all the time and support he needed for his career success. Now it's his wish to give me the time and support for what I wish to accomplish out of my life.**

**I ACCEPT HIS GIFT OF GIVING ME HIS ENERGY AND LOVE. NOW HE WILL SUPPORT MY TIME.**

We rejoice in the magnificence of our love.

# MAGNIFICENT LOVE

*(Author: Brent)*

The first thing that attracted me to Liz was her physical beauty.

More importantly, it was her worldly views that drew me in. She was different, expansive, and helped me view life with a much bigger lens than I had previously.

Liz is classy and she communicates very well. She speaks positively to me and to others.

She broadened our world and it was beautiful. I had no clue of the amazing relationship I was privileged to get with her.

She is intelligent, creative, and multitalented.

I love to hear her play the piano. She also plays the flute. How could I be so lucky.

Love is acts of service to each other.

Action is one of the biggest components for me. I can feel it and see it.

Liz shows her love to me with her steadfastness, her commitment, and patience.

There is a lot of noise in life. Liz is my North Star that brings me back.

She is my guiding light for what is really important. She quiets the noise.

We have built an unshakable trust over the years.

**I feel loved in our common bond and common values. We try to send this message to our children. It takes work and tenacity to get to this level of sacred love.**

**We are united in all ways.**

**What a beautiful life we have.**

**Thank you, Liz. I am in constant awe of it.**

**Our love is beyond my wildest dreams. Our love transformed into a magnificence I could never have dreamed possible.**

**She is my heart, my soul, and my joy.**

**WE ARE DEEPLY BONDED SOUL MATES NOW AND FOREVER.**

# LIVE AND LOVE WITHOUT REGRETS

*(Author: Brett)*

**Marrying Renee was the best thing that ever happened to me.**

**After a few false starts, I found that Renee was alone. I made contact with her. We had been junior high sweethearts, and I still was in love with her.**

**I appreciate the good human being she is. Renee respects me, which touches my heart as a man.**

**We take comfort in normal stuff. She and I are of the same nature. We have the same interests. I want her to be happy, and she wants me to be happy.**

**She gives me the gift that she wants to be with me and stays with me. We have been together for 20 years.**

**We both love and enjoy our dog, Marangi, and share the joy he brings to our life. We are a team and this shows up in designing and building our Barndominium together.**

**Renee told me that when she comes home and sees me, her heart still flutters. THAT IS WHY I LOVE RENEE.**

Love started in Jr. High and never waned.

# CAN I HAVE HEAVEN ON EARTH?

*(Author: Ann L)*

In my relationship with my mate, unfortunately he can only criticize me and harshly put me down, this erodes my confidence. The putdowns injure my very spirit. Unfortunately, he is stingy with his emotions.

But I yearn for that warm feeling of emotional safety; to be secure and protected and not have to be on guard.

I want the kind of love that has a warm feeling of acceptance so I can feel cherished. I have never had that from my parents or my mate. I fear failing in my relationship.

I want to be respected and know he has my back, that he would care for me. If we could spend loving time together, that would be heaven on earth.

I want to give my mate peace, humor, and a sense of security so it would boost his confidence. A low self-esteem causes a person to tear others down so they can feel superior. I want him to feel cherished.

I feel lost when he intentionally hurts me. I'd like to have easy, safe conversation. This feels like a desert, vacuous and barren. I am naturally a joyful spirit. I find love in abundance in my relationship with God, my friends and my family. Thus I fill my heart in other ways.

**My hope is strong for a harmonious, loving, and peaceful relationship with my husband in the future.**

**I HAVE SUCH A YEARNING TO GIVE MY LOVE.**

I find peace in giving love to my new dog.

# PERFECT LOVE IS ETERNAL

*(Author: Bliss)*

I prayed for a wife and Betty came along. It was love at first sight.

She was perfect for me, and I for her. We were perfect forever soul mates.

God is love, and He chose her for me. I proposed to her early in our relationship.

I need respect from her to feel loved, and I need affection.

My parents loved me but did not give me affection. Betty gave me that. We were friends. And that comforted me.

We never went to bed angry.

I didn't want to do anything to hurt Betty. If I did, I apologized immediately. My life's purpose was to make her happy.

Betty Unexpectedly died and I so miss her presence. I just want to be with her so much my heart aches. We were one. We complemented each other completely.

We worshiped together. God was first.

I accepted who Betty was and she accepted who I was.

There was no risk in our love. It only brought me joy. She was my joy.

**Our communication was open. We shared how we felt, it is not always simple, this made us both feel loved and cherished.**

**We wanted to please each other.**

**Perfect love is easy.**

**OUR LOVE IS FOREVER; IT IS ETERNAL.**

I prayed for a wife and along came Betty, my treasure my love. ❤

# ACCEPTANCE WINS LOVE

*(Author: Versita)*

I have been married three times. All of these relationships were cut short by unkind, painful divorce.

What I learned from this heartrending rejection created big chunks of doubt in myself. I did not trust myself to choose the right mate, someone who matched me.

Love is acceptance: to take me for who I am.

I should not have to alter who I am to get your love.

I should be able to feel safe and know my mate is in my corner.

Life has many ups and downs. I desire a mate who can give unconditional love.

We all want a mate that adores us, and we adore them back.

In my marriages, I did not have that unconditional love.

I am still waiting for my Boaz, for a love commitment.

I still yearn for truth, acceptance, and safety.

I WANT TO BE EMBRACED BY ARMS THAT WANT TO HOLD ME.

Where is my own Boaz?

# STRONG SILENT LOVE

*(Author: Susan)*

Love has so many faces.

My husband Tim loves me with a solid kind of love, and his passion is huge. He knows what I need without me telling him. Love is our companionship and I love him madly.

He is my favorite guy.

I had a knowing about Tim. That he was the right man for me. I didn't understand what love was before I married him. I now feel adored and cherished. I am his first priority.

He "gets" me, which is so comforting.

He's in tune with us; he is a really good man. He showed me what a family should be, I did not get that security from my own mother.

Tim is an excellent father. I never feared that he would abandon me.

He promised he would never leave me. He is a stabilizing force, and he is always there for me.

That's just who Tim is.

I enjoy his company and we spend a lot of time together. He just needs for me to be with him and he searches for ways to please me. I want to give him time together, being home together, and eating dinner together.

He is an awesome guy and he is my guy.

He wants my attention and presence, and I want Tim to feel he is my number one priority.

Our daughter has gone on to college. It is our time to create our "empty nest" future. I want him to be happy.

He looks out for me, yet I would like more physicality. I know Tim would give his life for me and I feel very grateful. He would do anything for our marriage; Tim is deep and his relationships run deep. He is very close to his family, and I never got to have that.

His friendships last a lifetime.

Tim is generous, kind and always ready to help in our family or a friend in need or a larger need of society. This makes me so proud of him. He is wicked smart, which attracted me to him in the first place.

Our family always comes first despite his very demanding executive duties. He is awesome and helps me be a better person. Tim encourages me in whatever I do. He is my partner in every sense of the word.

I ADMIRE TIM FOR ALL HE REPRESENTS.

Tim is my special guy.

# ENCHANTMENT OF AUTHENTICITY

*(Author: Don)*

**To me, love is to have as much compatibility and harmony as possible.**

**I loved to watch Linda "do" Linda. I took joy in seeing her authenticity. It was effortless and enchanting. I felt loved. My mate took pleasure in me being me. I was loved for who I am. There was no risk when I expressed my love. She completely supported me.**

**I gave all of myself to her. When Linda and I were apart, I missed being able to watch her. I just wanted to be with her all the time. Life was so easy. When she died, a piece of me died with her. LINDA ALWAYS SPOKE KINDLY TO ME.**

**I am happy now, and I love my present wife Diana. It will never be the same, but we have the ingredients to create a soulful relationship.**

**WE ARE CONSCIOUSLY KIND TO EACH OTHER.**

I was most myself under the glow of love.

# FAITHFUL AND TRUE LOVE

*(Author: Sidney & Shay)*

Many years ago, I got up on Christmas morning to prepare for my youngest son's birthday. I called out for my husband, his father, to join in the festivities but he was nowhere to be found. We got a call from him saying he was at a nearby hotel with his lover and would be back home after their encounter. It was a cruel thoughtless act, not only to our son but to me, his wife.

I was captured by his extraordinary gift as a piano player, that's all he had to offer. My work paid for our living expenses.

Through our divorce process I could hardly speak his name. My friend suggested we call him "Dumb Bucket." Which was very close to the sound of his name. You might as well have a little humor to soften the outlandish tragedy.

After many years of healing my disillusioned heart, Mike came into my life. There was an undeniable pull drawing us together.

Mike is almost everything my previous husband was not. He is a gentleman of integrity. He treats me with love, dignity and respect. Mike embraces my whole family. He is honorable, intelligent, and generous.

Though "dumb-bucket" mad me feel self-conscious, Mike taught me I could relax and be me.

**He naturally builds people up. Mike is faithful; I can trust him with my heart. His pure love offered so freely gives me peace. He has remained the same after 9 years of marriage. He has the greatest wish for my happiness. Mike's good wishes changed my view about distrusting men. He taught me to trust completely. I love him without question.**

**I AM TOTALLY SAFE IN MIKE'S ARMS**

Our love is forever, there is no end.

# UNCONDITIONAL LOVE

*(Author: Kathy)*

Love is always having my mate's back, and he has mine.

We keep difficult times between us. So, we don't try to get others to take sides. Neither one of us wants to injure the other.

Harlan often knows what I need before I can voice it.

There is absolute trust between us. It is inconceivable to believe we would not have that trust.

He makes me feel that I am special to him when he takes genuine interest in what is important to me. Like my creativity and making beautiful handbags.

He compliments me and encourages my creativity.

He cares about the inner me and what I take pride in.

We share the joy in the son we have together and that is special.

I want to give Harlan unconditional love and encourage him to do what he loves. And he wants to give me the same.

We share our spiritual life, and that is critical to our partnership and love.

I miss him when we are apart, and if we don't get to speak with each other, when we do come together it's

**exciting and fresh. He cares about what I care about and that makes me feel important.**

**THIS REFRESHMENT BRINGS ENERGY TO OUR UNION.**

Harlan and I have each other's back, I want to protect him as much as he wants to protect me.

# SWEET CONSCIOUS LOVE

*(Author: Kym)*

I believe in love. Love is compassion, friendship, honesty, attraction, and gentleness.

I love my husband Zack with all my heart. He is very compassionate and gentle. We have a lot of fun together. We use loving sarcasm to playfully express our feelings.

I need my nighttime kisses. Zack kisses me 3 times on my lips, 3 kisses on my eyes, one kiss on the tip of my nose, and one kiss on my forehead. He covers me with kisses, and I feel adored, all gooey and warm on the inside.

I really admire Zack's strength, and he is my "calm" in stressful waters. I am also very proud for his military service. He was a Ranger in the army. He is capable of protecting us from danger and I feel very safe.

My heart sings with joy since we have started our spiritual journey. Peace and joy have added color to our life. It is hard to describe the depth and solid dimension it has added to all aspects of our marriage.

My hope for our future is to grow old with Zack. I want to create the kind of loving relationship I witnessed in my grandparents.

We are well on our way. Zack does so many personal and intimate things for me that make my heart beat

**faster. He likes to wash my long hair and braid it for me. He massages my feet after a busy day. He often helps by washing the dishes after I've made him a delicious dinner.**

**On a bigger scale, he adopted my son and one of my daughters, who took his name. He will also adopt another daughter.**

**ZACK GOES BEYOND MY DREAM COME TRUE**

We fell head over heels in love.

# THE PURE LOVE OF A BABY IS MYSTICAL

*(Author: Sidney, Leeaigh and Makese)*

**They had a beautiful brand new baby. Her name is Analea.**

**Both Makese and Leeaigh want to give their baby girl the gift of a family unit. A bond that offers security now and in the future.**

**The whole deal. A mother, a daddy, and a big sister, Alora.**

**It is obvious how much both parents love their new, precious daughter.**

**Love has brought them together and love has set into motion the actions to create a strong, loving, family unit.**

**Love isn't always easy. They cared and unselfishly loved enough to work all this out.**

**WONDER OF WONDERS.**

**LOVE CONQUERS ALL OBSTACLES.**

Makese, Leeaigh, Analea, and Alora are Creating a happy, whole family.

...and a few broken on the way

# COMMITMENT TO OUR PROMISES

*(Author: Todd)*

I first met Paula when we were in Bible College. She was a student and I was the Professor's Assistant.

Her boldness to standup for her beliefs and her commitment to her faith is what immediately attracted me to her. It made her sparkle with energy.

I knew I loved Paula shortly after I graduated. I was getting ready to start my first assignment. We had been dating for two months. The realization that I was in love gave me a happy secure feeling in my heart.

Love to me is keeping the promises we made and doing what we said we would do.

I love Paula's passion, it is contagious; I love her commitment to her beliefs. I love how she loves our grandchildren and our son Caleb. I am grateful to be on this life journey with her.

Perfection is not our goal, but commitment to our promises is. We are there for each other even in the roughest times. Including the time a hit-and-run driver left her unconscious in the hospital. I witnessed her struggle to remember her loved ones. I feared the unknown and the possibility that memories of me might disappear from her mind as well.

**Paula shows her love for me in the small things, by taking care of our grandchildren and helping our son Caleb.**

**To feel loved, I want and need her to stay the course on our life together and to care about my needs.**

**The last words I want Paula to hear me say are, "I LOVE YOU AND I'LL SEE YOU IN ETERNITY."**

I Paula will give you the gift of doing what I told you I would do.

I Todd will always protect you and buy you lots of candles.

# MY UNMOVABLE ANCHOR

*(Author: Paula)*

**I believe love is many actions: protecting and trusting each other.**

**Todd tells me, "I will always be here for you. You can trust me and I will take care of you." And he does, physically, mentally, and emotionally.**

**I love him for his traits of loyalty, honesty, and trustworthiness.**

**He is nonjudgmental and accepts me for who I am. Another important trait is he also accepts my family.**

**Todd has the ability to see the bigger picture when I can't at times, and he helps me to see it with him.**

**He loves the Lord with everything in him. He loves to serve God and will always be a student of the Lord. Todd is an exceptionally great father and grandfather.**

**He has phenomenal instincts. When things are confusing or out of control, he brings order and calm.**

**Todd goes the extra mile. He knows how to love me in practical ways. I loved candles and when we were shopping I was sniffing all the different aromas, he noticed my sniffing and bought me all the candles in the case. Small gestures like this make me feel cherished.**

**Though he is very busy as a pastor, we have breakfast together every morning. It is our special time.**

As a young child I lived in Germany with my parents. They bought me a Steiff Stuffed dog. I loved it and carried it everywhere with me. I lost it and was devastated. Todd heard that story. He searched for years until he found one for me in Germany and had it shipped to me.

All these things confirm that he loves and adores me.

When he is away, I immediately miss his solidness. Todd is my anchor. I live with a lot of pain from my accident, and he understands my physical, mental, and emotional struggles.

I am grateful God gave me Todd. We are doing life together and healing each other's old wounds.

TODD IS MY BIGGEST CHEERLEADER. THAT EXHILARATES ME.

# SOULFUL CONNECTION

*(Author: Anonymous)*

I lost the love of my life to cancer; the following is part of a letter I wrote to him the day before he died:

"This love I have for you is unlike anything I've experienced before. It brewed and bubbled, rose and fell, aged and transformed, it became the deepest connection I've ever felt with a man… and you with a woman. I can't explain how or why it happened, but I know you and I were supposed to meet when we did and take this journey together.

Our love expanded to fill the old cracks, and we opened to new possibilities. Perhaps there's something about "old love" that makes minutes precious.

We've wound up giving each other the greatest gift one can receive… unconditional love. With it comes the knowledge that we're whole and good just the way we are. Our lives have meant something. The long-standing doubt faded away. Our experience of love was born of wisdom.

Even though cancer cut short living out our lives together, it opened the possibility for a deep, trusting friendship. A purer kind of love with deep attachment.

I want to thank you for what you've given me. You know me, you see me, you feel me, you take great care in being with me. I feel safe letting down my guard, knowing I don't need to be in control anymore. I feel fully known, trusted and respected for who I am. And I know you feel the same.

You are a precious gift. I will never be the same. I had to find myself before I could find you. You will never leave my heart; you will live there forever."

My experience with this first love broke me open. Forced a deep self-examination. My ego had expectations that prevented the free flow of soulful love. It kept me from knowing and accepting a man for who he was VS. what I wanted him to be. This never allowed me to reveal the vulnerable parts of me, which needed to be honored, respected, loved and cherished.

That year was a year of surrendering. I dedicated myself to giving him the most peaceful time of his life, I experienced feeling even more love than I gave. The devastating loss turned out to be the gift.

These experiences led to an even more powerful expression of Big Soulful Love with my current love. Whom I will spend the rest of my life with.

IT TOOK THE BIGGEST LOSS IN MY LIFE TO BRING ME THE BIGGEST LOVE OF MY LIFE.

# THE MIRACLE OF LOVE

*(Author: Janie)*

I realized at the young age of 5 years old I had no one to take care of me. My father was an alcoholic and a womanizer; my mother was riddled with fear and needed someone to take care of her.

We were neighbors with the Bellairs Family. They lived across the lake from us.

I would look over at their family outings with my binoculars. Their parents took Bobby on their boat to water ski and they ate together. I knew at that early age, that was what I wanted. Bobby was 7 and I was 5 years old; we were always good friends.

Loving is ever-growing, we would do anything for each other. Our love was meant to be.

We listen to each other, and we care. I respect Bobby a great deal and he respects me. That is very important in our relationship.

We are each other's lifeline. We have been in love for 72 years. I knew the life I did not want. He pulled me out of it and rescued me.

We were like one person, and always in contact with each other. You couldn't get a thin piece of paper between us, that's how close we are. I am blessed that our life is so magical and always has been.

**Most important is that we hug and kiss each other and hold hands even when we go to bed.**

**I am amazed that we keep loving each other even more as life goes on. Bobby saved me when I was a little girl, and now he has dementia and I am caring for him.**

**So now it is my turn to save him, we put our marriage first, we found someone we could not live without in each other. We know that everyone in our life has a purpose for us and is worth something.**

**I love to live in the light of our love. A good humor is important. We know what each other thinks.**

**I WILL BE BY BOBBY'S SIDE TO THE VERY END.**

**WE ARE A MIRACLE.**

As a prima ballerina I, Janie, danced mostly for my love.

# WE MADE A SACRED PROMISE

*(Author: Ginny)*

**The love I feel for my husband Kevin is encapsulated IN OUR PROMISE. We promised to love each other no matter what is going on. There is no place for rejection in our union. We commit to this promise through the good times, and the not so good times, which are here now. Kevin was in an accident, and his health is a huge challenge now. That promise gets us through these times.**

**We might be angry with each other, struggling with life, but there is still a solid background of love. God is good. He is the pinnacle of our union. He created marriage so we could understand love. We are the earthly version of God's love. Christ went to the cross for us. He gave us life with His death. Kevin and I are willing to die for each other. No matter what is happening, we stick together and trust in each other. It is a choice, and we choose the gift of love.**

**LOVE TRULY IS A GIFT, AND IT COMES FROM GOD. HE IS THE AUTHOR.**

Ginny and Kevin, our promise

# TELENOVELA LOVE STORY

*(Author: Alex)*

For me, love is understanding my place in the world.

My first true love was my high school sweetheart. We had several mystical adventures together.

Something changed after we had been married for a while. I felt as if we belonged together like best friends, yet she did not feel the same way.

I did not share her experience; I still felt the same love which kept me hopeful and in my "place."

When our world was disturbed by external problems we were overwhelmed and she told me she wanted to leave me.

This shattered my heart and my whole existence. I was blown away when I realized her feelings had changed but mine had not.

I was lost in my self-pity. But I could not stay in that sorry state of helplessness. I distracted myself with work, my university, and stayed away from intimate relationships. They were dangerous to me.

Miraculously I now allow myself to be in an intimate relationship with a partner that fills my soul.

She is self-reflective, she has the courage to examine herself trying to find the real woman inside.

Her energy and her beingness drew me towards her. I feel we are compatible because we share the same sensitivity for each other and the world around us.

We have many common interests and values which magnetically pull us toward each other.

We are struggling with a forbidden love because I am free, but she is not free yet. These hard circumstances are treated with tenderness and kindness by her.

She is honest with me, and I appreciate the way she can do it with gentleness and love. She cares for me enough to not ever want to hurt me.

The passion has been so strong. We have stopped to look for other connections that broadens and go beyond that; passion in our experiences, passion in our work, and finding better ways to communicate.

The type of love I have with her is one of the purest forms of love I have ever experienced, despite us feeling like living inside a Telenovela love story (Mexican Soap Opera).

For now, our love has to remain unrequited until the circumstances allow us to be in our right space for this world. WE CARE FOR EACH OTHER'S GOOD WITH EQUAL INTENSITY.

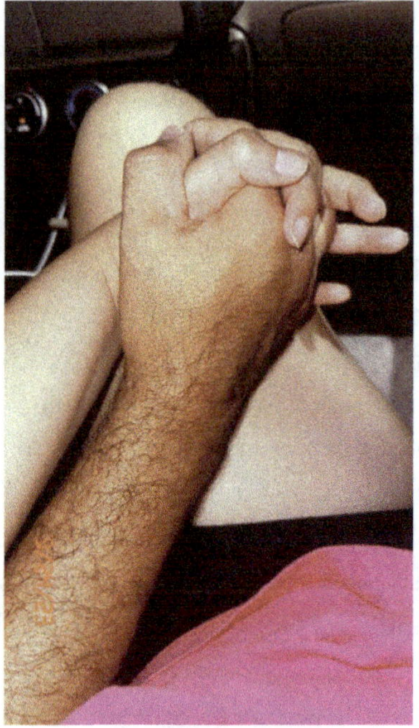

We hold on to each other for our healing.

# SACRIFICE FOR LOVE

*(Author: Sheila)*

**Sheila was not lucky in love, but she should win an Oscar for her role as a Mother.**

**She single handedly raised her well-adjusted son Nathan. When Sheila discovered he had a natural talent for drums, she gave him his first set when he was only 1 year old.**

**She nurtured his passion. Sheila sacrificed her needs for his needs. This allowed her to send Nathan to the Boston School of Music. Nathan finished the schooling and his talent as a drummer won him gigs all across America.  Tours takes him to many European countries. Sheila's pride and delight in his success made it all worthwhile.**

**Sheila also taught Nathan how to successfully handle his finances and business deals. HER TRAITS OF SACRIFICE, SINGLE MINDEDNESS AND UNCONDITIONAL LOVE MAKES HER A BEAUTIFUL FACSIMILE OF PERFECT LOVE.**

Sheila inspired Nathan to go for the stars

# REFUGE OF PRECIOUS LOVE

*(Author: Kerry)*

I see and feel love as support, nurturing, and caring physically and emotionally for each other.

This is not only in the good, easy times, but also in the hard times.

Neil is always on my side. He remembers the little things that are important to me: like my birthday and events that matter.

I need Neil to listen to me and remember my needs.

He listens to me without trying to fix me.

The risk in love is that if I give wholly of myself and he does not receive me, what else can I give? He has always minimized this risk.

Neil is always cooking for us and maintaining our home.

He takes care of his health and is involved with mine. This creates such softness in my heart for him.

If we have to be apart, I feel the disconnect and my anxiety heightens.

My anxiety inflates and I feel emotionally off kilter. I am no longer centered.

Neil and I clung to each other when death took our beloved son Eric. Our world broke, but we were pulled together and magnetized by the strength of our love.

**He listens to me without scolding me for my thoughts.**

**NEIL IS MY REFUGE AND MY SAFE SHELTER.**

Neil and Kerry have a Laugh Out Loud joyful life.

# THE SHADOW OF OUR LOVE

*(Author: Neil)*

**Love is emotional for me. I love the feeling I get when Kerry is there for me. I always want to be in Kerry's glow. I can't get enough of her. Physical contact thrills me. I can see love in her face, and it makes me feel like a man. She wants to be with me, desired and wanted. If being in an exclusive relationship with physical contact is considered codependency, then I want to be codependent with her.**

**I love to be desired and wanted by Kerry.**

**We give our all to each other.**

**To overhear her brag on me or say loving things about our relationship melts my heart.**

**It calms me when I know for sure Kerry loves me. And loves us.**

**When we are not together, I feel emotionally fragile and want the closeness of our love.**

**KERRY IS MY HEARTTHROB.**

# ON TOP OF THE WORLD

*(Author: Dave)*

**Love is commitment, commitment to care for each other's emotional and spiritual wellbeing and safety. There are lots of days I don't feel like nurturing, but I make a commitment to do it anyway. Loving is easy, living it is tougher.**

**It's about the little things. Karen's little gifts of love so sweetly given touch my heart. Like good meals, doing my laundry and SEEING ME.**

**Love is about listening. I really hear Karen and she hears me.**

**When Karen says to me "you're a great husband and hugs me, I'm on top of the world".**

**We must have trust in all forms. I trust Karen will always do the right things for me and our family.**

**SHE GIVES COMFORT TO MY SOUL.**

**We are still happily married after 30 years, communicating is easy, and we spend a lot of time talking to each other. Love is time and time is love.**

**We have warm feelings for each other. Karen tells me she wants to be special to me and she is.**

**We write to each other in a love journal. To find someone you can trust is not easy, but I trust Karen.**

**My love requires a high level of acceptance from my mate. We need to be able to help each other work out our hurts and pains from our youths.**

**I want Karen to feel her value.**

**SHE IS WORTH THE WHOLE WORLD TO ME.**

# DATES AT HOME DEPOT

*(Author: Karen)*

Love is so many things.

In the beginning, it is feeling-based and more emotional. Over times it shifts to more action based. Mine and Dave's choices are made based on those feelings, and we appreciate each other.

It is sort of like making Jell-O. In the beginning it is watery and splashes around, then it solidifies and becomes firm. The ingredients are still the same but become firmer into a different state. That is why mine and Dave's relationship has worked so successfully. We gel together and have become solidified.

To feel loved, I need eye contact, purposeful conversation, kindness, and acceptance. There must be trust and consistency. I want to be witnessed by Dave.

I feel cherished when he writes me letters in our love journal. When he notices the internal me and SEES me.

I love to fill in those empty spaces he missed in his childhood so he can feel complete. We can heal each other of those old hurts. It would be very difficult to get through a childhood without a wounded self-esteem. It is a constant peeling off layers of hurt from the past.

I feel safe when Dave listens without comment and tries to understand. He really hears me.

**When he is not around I miss his companionship, his kindness, and his talkativeness. He is truly my best friend; I love how we joke around with each other. We joked that we had dates in home depot, his chatter makes it a lot of fun. DAVE IS MY TRUE LOVE.**

Dave and Karen took each other to the mountain top.

# LOVE IN UNEXPECTED PLACES

*(Author: Brian)*

In the beginning when I first thought I was in love the relationship broke and we were no longer coupled. I made the decision to prepare myself to be the kind of person that would attract the kind of mate I desired.

So, what I learned is that love is when two people are completely committed to each other. When we serve each other's needs.

Love is being a helper and a companion with no conditions. It is when I am able to fully open myself to someone. It is when I can be completely myself without fear of judgement.

I opened my heart and felt like I was ready to give myself to a special other and receive from someone who was ready to give to me.

I attended a friend's wedding and noticed Kelsey, an old friend from high school. We had lost touch. When I saw her at the wedding, I knew I wanted to say hi and see how she had been. A little electrical shock ignited, and I knew I wanted to date her.

On our very first date, I discovered her fun-loving personality, how easily she laughed, and it didn't hurt that she was absolutely gorgeous.

The more time I spent with her, the more I realized she is the salt of the earth kind of woman with a heart of gold.

Am I in love with her? Yes, I am absolutely in love with her. She makes it really easy. Our love is reciprocal.

I feel loved when Kelsey listens to me and really hears me. She expresses her love for me both emotionally and physically with kind expressions and gentle touches.

We are excited to be with each other. We see the good in each other. We recognize our effort and good qualities. We encourage ourselves to improve on shortcomings in a friendly way, with acceptance.

Kelsey is inquisitive and shows her love by listening to me. She wants to know what my needs are.

She expresses how much I mean to her and how much she loves me. She wants to spend time with me and be a part of my life.

Whether it's her words or actions, I am constantly reminded how she feels about me and how much she truly cares about me.

OUR LOVE IS MY BIGGEST BLESSING, I WILL LOVE HER FOREVER.

Brian said, "When Kelsey came back into my life, I knew I was blessed with the magic of love".

# GLUED TOGETHER BY SOULFUL LOVE

*(Author: David)*

Allison and I met at orientation at the University of Michigan. I fell in love with her pretty quickly. She had a tender personality that made me want to feel that softness. We have been happily married for 39 years.

Our relationship can be defined by a gentle commonality. Love for us includes a desire to make each other's dreams come true.

We also have this same hope for our 2 daughters, Haley and Jessie. We want to help them achieve their dreams too.

Allison and I share our faith and are committed to our common values. The sound of her voice soothes me.

We love our many adventurous vacations with our daughters. The time spent together breathes fun and love into our complete family. It revitalizes and refreshes us. Our roles as parents complement each other's. She runs the family and is a great mother. And I provide our living.

I feel her love and commitment when she helps at my Healthy Choices Seminars by selling the books I write on Wholistic Living. This behavior tells me she believes in me. That boosts my ego as the man in her life. She supports me in all ways.

Our most important job is to raise healthy, happy, well-adjusted daughters. We take this very seriously and she encourages me to stay on track.

When I first started practicing as an M.D., I was quickly disillusioned by the lack of healthy improvements in my patients. I came home one day and announced to Allison, "I QUIT!" She rapidly responded, "You can't quit, you've got student loans to pay off!"

Well, she was right about that reality. I partnered with 2 other doctors who shared the same disappointments. We started the Wholistic Medicine clinic. Patients came through the door by the hundreds. I had to stop taking new patients after a while to preserve giving my family the time and attention we all deserve. Together we help thousands of patients experience health they hadn't felt before. But we still take the family time we need that we all treasured.

Allison and I had a common dream for our daughters to be prepared for a fruitful life which fulfilled them. They both got their undergrad from the University of Michigan and then went to medical school.

At this moment in time, Haley and Jessie both work with me in the clinic. There is such joy and pride in this. Common goals are a strong glue for our family.

With the present antisemitism we are faced with the reality that our girls might be harmed. So, Allison and I work very hard to protect them and keep them safe.

We are not only successful in our support for each other, but as a family we take care of each other. We get to make a meaningful contribution to society. And this makes all of us happy and fulfilled.

# ALLISON IS MY FOREVER SOULMATE

When he saw her, he was hooked by love's sweet promise.

Dr. B has given a great quality of life to others.

# MAJSETIC LOVE IS ETERNAL

*(Authors: Becky & Sidney)*

What an example of everlasting love Becky and Don's love portrays. I can sum it up in one incident.

Becky worked in my department, and I already knew her to be a splendid young woman. She and Don had been dating and knew they wanted to get married. They were freshly out of college, and their lives glistened brightly before them. Life was their happy oyster.

That particular weekend, they joined a friend who was also from Ohio (Go Buckeyes!) for a quick turnaround trip so they could all visit their parents.

On their way home, a dark, shrouded night hid many dangers. Becky was sitting on Don's lap, and the driver fell into a deep sleep. They crashed in a devastating, life-threatening accident.

Becky's head hit the windshield, and they were all twisted into a tangled mess before the Corvette trembled and eerily came to a quiet stop. They were taken to a hospital in Michigan.

Becky and Don hung by a fragile thread, drifting between life and death.

Because of her multiple head and facial injuries, Becky's whole head and face were wrapped like a mummy.

The day finally came when the doctors would perform the unveiling and painstakingly remove the bandages. A gasp escaped into the room, and they advised her not to look in a mirror. Her face was swollen, there was damage to her eye, and a major cut on her cheek had gone through a nerve. Don and Becky maintained their strong faith in God. This comforted and sustained them.

Becky insisted on going into the bathroom to look in the mirror. A shocked silence hovered in the air. Then the silence burst into peals of laughter. Becky called out, "I've got to go show Don!"

She ran into his room, and he proclaimed, "You are the most beautiful woman I've ever seen!"

As her employer and friend, I had been checking on her regularly. She told me Don's reaction, and I told her, "Honey, you need to marry this guy as quick as you can. He's a keeper."

I believe she already knew that Don looked at her through the eyes of love and saw only the woman he loved looking back at him with radiance and beauty.

Becky and Don have been married for over 30 years and have four grown children.

This one incident revealed a love so deep and so grounded that it was a miracle of ETERNAL SOULFUL LOVE.

Becky and Don let their love guide them to its purest form.

# LOVE IN THE TWINKLING OF AN EYE

*(Author: Sidney & Janco)*

JANCO, had a business offering adrenaline rush experiences in the South African Bush. He was handsome, with a knockout physique. And was himself an untamed bundle of adrenaline. At this time in his life, he had never given his heart to another.

A friend told him, "I think I just saw your perfect love match!" Janco perked up, "O really and who might that be?" The friend just told him, "Follow me and I will show you your mystery love."

They were in a small village, so it was not far. They ended up standing in front of a large window to an African Travel/Safari Agency. The moment Janco saw the travel agent, he rushed inside and asked her for her name.

She told him her name a little reluctantly. After all, he was a complete stranger.

He grabbed her hand and said, "Listen here Henriette, we are going to get married, but I have to go to Europe for a year. You are to wait for me and be prepared for our wedding when I return."

True to a story book romance, the conquering hero returned claimed his woman and they married.

And now for the rest of the intrigue. Janco became a Safari Guide. They moved to a lodge that Henriette would manage.

They had their only child Shana. Janco had a successful Guide business but there was one little kink. It was not unusual for female clients to fall in love with the Safari Guide, much less a hunk of a dream man like Janco. He has a mystical testosterone energy about him.

Henriette was on fire with burning jealousy. She confronted Janco. He told her, "jealousy is your problem and I have no doubt where my love and loyalty are". He finished with, "you must fix this in your heart because it is not in mine".

The summation of their story is that they have been happily married for over 20 dramatic, loving and caring years. What I learned is that love is when two people are completely committed to each other and serve as each other's partner.

Love is being a helper and a companion with no conditions. It is when you are able to be fully open with another. It is when you can be completely yourself. WE MUST ACCEPT EACH OTHER FOR WHAT WE ARE, AND LIVE THAT TRUTH.

Janco is showing us the dragon lizard on the Safari.

Janco and his wife Henriette.

# WHAT DO YOU DO WHEN YOUR SOULMATE DIES?

The second Christmas without Wayne I felt like I was adrift on a lonely planet.

**The feeling of being left behind was apocalyptically painful. All the joy and love from my children and grandchildren around me could not fill that emptiness. That void wasn't created by them but by the absence of Wayne. I no longer had someone who belonged to me, just me, and who I belonged to. The space around me felt like a gigantic distance separating me from the real world. It felt like an empty barrier surrounding me, which could not be penetrated. No one else could even come close to giving me what my heart needed. While no one else could even remotely fill the cavernous emptiness. I am grateful with all my heart for what I had with Wayne, but this emptiness is so deep, there is nothing that can fill it up. The hope I have now is that I can replace this emptiness with loving memories.**

# A LONELY PLANET

*(Author: Sidney)*

Dated 12/24/21,

*Letter to Wayne six months after he passed.*

Dearest Wayne,

It is your first birthday we have been apart, and the open space is painfully empty. I yearn to see you and hold you once more.

Your grandchildren miss you. Kym still tears up at the mention of your name. I know Paul and Mary Ann miss you very much. I loved and love you beyond explanation.

Though I am comfortable in my new home, it is only a waiting station until I am with you once more. I miss your tender smile and your eloquent words of love. I want to be embraced by your hugs warm with acceptance. Just being in the same space together.

WHO COULD EVER CONCEIVE WHAT IT IS LIKE TO LOSE YOUR SOULMATE? It has left a hole as big as the sky.

Though I knew how lucky I was to have you, I cherished every moment we had together. I did not know the depth and breadth of you as my treasure. You completed me. It is a lonely planet indeed without you.

I truly gave my heart and soul to you, my darling Wayne. Nothing was held back from either one of us.

**Only in one lifetime could a person be the recipient of such love and devotion of this magnitude.**

**I loved you. I adored you. I spent my total self on loving you. You were the pinnacle of what was possible. Your devotion gave me such security and serenity.**

**I have been so grateful because of your honest and true nature. You gave me the amazing gift of being able to trust men, and I am grateful. Our spiritual union filled my quest to know God more deeply.**

**You promised you'd be just inside the gates of heaven on your golden folding chair to be the first to greet me when I showed up. I look forward to experiencing *Agape* love with you. I love you eternally Wayne,**

**Sidney**

We looked into each other eyes. Found that little wounded creature that only we could heal. You could heal me and I could heal you.

# LOVE LETTERS FROM OUR HEARTS

Dear Readers,

I want to share mine and Wayne's LOVE STORY. Perhaps it will give you ideas as you pursue your own quest.

Across our 41 ½ years of marriage, Wayne and I poured out our feelings in OUR love journals.

These feelings have kept me in touch with the magic we shared in a fulfilling life of tenderness and fearless LOVE.

I feel Wayne's presence with me every time I gaze on a photo of us. LOVE speaks to us louder than words.

His voice was a melody of feelings, and I was captured by all expressions of our committed LOVE. It wasn't complicated.

OUR LOVE WAS REAL AND WE BUILT EACH OTHER UP. LOVE is looking at your mate and seeing another soul and seeing them looking back at you.

Our eyes are the window to the person we are deep within.

When we look deeply into our mate's eyes without words, we see the scared little being that desperately wants someone to LOVE and accept them. Pride is not allowed to sit at our table. Joyful acceptance is our welcomed, permanent, and honored guest.

It takes unbelievable bravery to hand over your exposed heart to another.

LOVE IS WORTH ALL THE RISKS!

May 26th

Dearest Sidney,

You are a nice lady! I was thinking how respectfully you used the language. Your speech is never coarse but always honorable and respectful.

I see how caring you are with your mother, and it reminds me how caring you are toward everyone. I need your care. You are in your divine Self most of the time. I'm sure that's why quality women like Ginny, Liz, Gail, Patty, Susan, etc., etc., etc., are attracted to you. That's one of the many reasons I'm attracted to you.

You're my special one and my lover and my partner in everything. I love you Sidney.

You're trustful and loving,

Wayne

Every day was as thrilling as our wedding day.

May 29, 2002

Dearest Wayne:

My soul has found your soul and our energy has become one. I know you are the one that God sent to me. I could not live my life without you. Each sunset, each ray of sun, each bird song, each joy in life is meaningful because I have you to love and receive your love. It is forever and I promise you my never-ending love.

I respect you; I delight in you, I feel loved by you. Thank you for all your dedication.

I love you deeply,
Sidney

September 2, 2002

Dear Sidney,

I am so glad to be home because we'll be together again in a couple of hours. I don't do well without you. For sure we complement each other in many ways. I cannot describe the many ways. There are no words for you.

I feel vital and connected and safe and cared for and believed in. There's nothing more to be needed. You are my sunrise, my joy, and my every thought. I too am glad we found each other in this lifetime. This was our time; you're it.

I love you passionately,
Wayne

Dear Wayne,

It has been such a great fun dreaming, researching, going to fireplace stores and furniture stores with you in our pursuit of our Charleston bedroom. You have a beautiful romantic heart. It has been so difficult for me to trust. You are breaking down those barriers and helping me learn that I can trust.

Thank you for being the man that you are. Someone I can admire, count on, love, and feel safe with. Also, you are a heck of a great lover. Wow, you make me feel wanted and desirable. It will be peaceful contentment falling asleep in your arms. We will enjoy our Charleston room, the warm reflection of our fire. And we will embrace under the beauty of our canopy bed.

I love you deeply Wayne,

Sidney

Dear Sidney,

I feel intensely connected to you. My spirit is in perfect harmony with your spirit. I want more than anything to be helpful to you, to be a positive force for you, and for you to feel always that you can count on me. I hold you in a high place of honor. There is not one aspect of you that I am disappointed in. I like your every living habit. I am so very proud of you as a person and a woman! I love to introduce you to others then watch their reaction. You are impressive and I love it!

I love you forever!

Wayne

**My dearest Wayne,**

**You truly are my hero. It really scared me and made me sad about my eye. You took charge and went into immediate action. Then you committed to do the hard job of moving so I wouldn't have to be stressed. Thank you from the bottom of my heart. You do so much that makes you my hero.**

**Getting up at 3:00 AM to fix my computer proved your patience and kindness.**

**Hooking up all of our new equipment.**

**Celebrating Brett's job with him endeared you to me. I appreciate you, admire you, your capabilities and intelligence, and love your optimism.**

**I love you Wayne. You're mine for life,**

**Sidney**

Together Forever.

**Dear Sidney,**

**I love your "Let's see what's over the next hill" attitude. Your quest for adventure is always tempered with thoughtfulness in the search for the good. I feel totally accepted and appreciated by you. I feel safe with you, so I wish to be with you as much as possible. I can always count on you to do your share.**

**At Elkhart you worked like a beaver making the move. You never shrink back when effort is required. I love your spirit.**

**I am totally at peace when we sit next to each other in church. I love your devotion and trust in our God.**

**I love you fiercely,**

**Wayne**

September 3rd, 2003,

My darling husband Wayne,

We've done another first with each other. It was a thrilling venture to travel around the United States with the man I love. You were always ready to go on the next adventure. You enjoy them as much as I do. There was such a joy in experiencing the top of Crazy Horse with you, to go on the same walk in his footsteps together.

Thank you for your thoughtfulness and leaving me to be alone a few minutes so I could cry out to God, the great mystery. We beat as one heart and thrill to the same experiences. I could not ask for more than this to experience the world with my one true love. You are my best friend, my partner, my love.

I love you deeply, Wayne,

Sidney

We were connected with touch and soul.

**September 22, 2003, Around USA 2 months**

**Dearest Sidney,**

**Our tour of this beautiful country was memorable because of your appreciation of God's creation and the spirit we encountered in the West. Every time my heart and soul are touched I look at you and you're touched too. I know you are feeling the same as I do even when words fail. There were so many occasions of the "oneness" of our spirit; the connection that binds us together that we can experience but cannot express in words.**

**Our challenge of restoring your vision triggered a fierce campaign in me to beat the force that is challenging your vision. I will fight it with all my might; I won't rest until it is completely defeated. I will NEVER, NEVER give in.**

**I love you Sidney,**

**Wayne**

Dear Wayne,

It just gets better and sweeter with each passing day. I feel like our life has been a great adventure of fun, exploration, unbelievable accomplishments, spiritual and peaceful. It is like walking around in a dream.

I was profoundly touched when you put Jacob's little burp bag on my pillow. You know how much I love him; the joy he brings my heart and it just made that a magnificent gesture of love. You never hesitate or complain about taking me to see him. I thank you so much for that. It is just another piece of evidence of your devotion and love.

I feel more secure with you than I ever have. You are my one true love, and I am devoted to you.

I love you, Wayne.

Sidney

We love our little grandson Jacob.

**Dear Sidney,**

**My sense of oneness with you is total and permeates every fiber of me. There are a few moments when I forget you are other and think of you as another part of me. It's like I don't see where I leave off and you begin; I am unaware of a boundary.**

**I usually know how you feel about things because it's how I'm feeling about them. I thoroughly enjoyed our western journey. Our combined spirits and adventure made everything we did a special joy. We're pulled in the same direction. Our auto pilots have the same settings. You're my priority.**

**I love you, Sidney, forever and ever.**

**Wayne.**

**AND THEY LIVED HAPPILY EVER AFTER.**

Our love was as exciting and thrilling as petting a cheetah, lion or elephant.

November 1st, 2004

Dear Wayne,

The last few days you have been especially sweet and tender. I can see the love and caring in your eyes. It has made me feel cherished, wanted, loved, and protected. It is a gift that I really need from you, so I feel more and more secure. Thank you.

It is fun to flirt with you. I feel like a schoolgirl around you at times. I love our growing bond and friendship. We will grow old together, but I won't see your wrinkles. I'll be looking for the gleam in your eyes.

I love you as my soulmate,

Sidney.

2005

Dearest of all Friends-

Early this morning before I got out of bed, I heard you greeting Jacob on the front porch. It was the sound of unbounded love and joy. I'm so proud of the kind of grandmother you are. You are the kind that years from now Jacob will recall that "Grandma truly loved and cared for me, she made me feel worthy and special."

Working with you on this past Couple's Empowerment was a beautiful experience and a reminder of how very many constructive projects we've worked on together. It started in Value Engineering and shows no sign of stopping. We're one heck of a team.

I love you Sidney,

Wayne

Dear Wayne,

Each day I wake up to see you next to me I am thrilled and thankful to God. Life is brighter more colorful and has more meaning because I get to live it with you. When I consider all that we have already experienced, I am amazed and it fills my heart with joy to be able to share this journey with you my soulmate. I can't imagine it any other way now.

And looking towards the future is still exciting knowing we get to face it together. Each new day with you is like a new beginning. You fill me up and I so appreciate the effort you make in our relationship. You are my one true love.

I love you deeply,

Sidney

We did everything together even elephants.

**June 26, 2005**

**Dear Sidney,**

**I love you as a warrior loves. When I look at you, I see your precious vulnerable soul that powerfully attracts me to protect and care for you. I am the one who will shield you from life's harshness and danger. If need be, should any unexpected disaster overtake us, I'd gladly go back to work to support and care for you. With me you shall always have a safe home. I want to do whatever needs to be done to make a safe, peaceful, and fulfilling life for you. I shall always be your safe harbor.**

**God has blessed me with the strength and capabilities, and I gladly use them to care for you.**

**I love you fiercely,**

**Wayne**

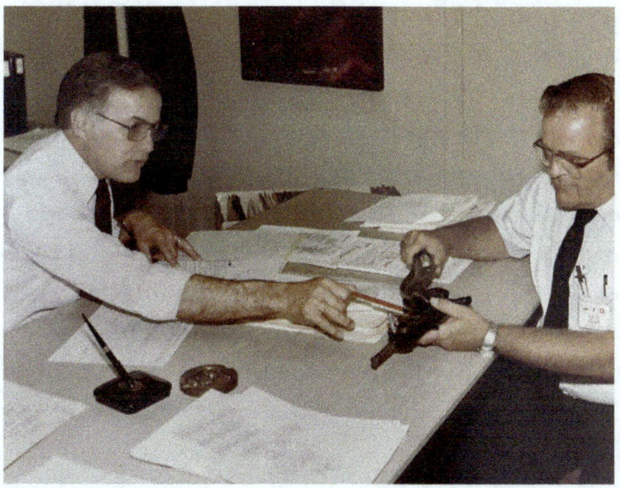

Wayne was Sidney's Boaz.

Dear Wayne,

Thank you for the luscious poinsettia plant. I turned around and a little shock of love ran to my heart. I love your expression of tenderness and love. It makes me feel cherished and important in your world. You are my one and only. You make my existence full of glory and hope. I love to be near you to touch you and to be touched by you. I treasure our closeness.

I love you Wayne,
Sidney

My dearest Sidney,

I feel so honored to have you as my wife. Every guy hopes to get that one-in-a-million girl: beautiful, sexy, intelligent, capable, productive, and wanted by all the other guys. You're that girl and I got you. My wildest dream came true. God obviously loves me to bless me with you.

Sitting beside you in church is the most spiritual relationship imaginable while worshiping. He had created it all. Wow! Words fail but the peace and correctness I experienced with you goes beyond reason. I never want it to end, and it won't. I would be so pleased if both my daughters were exactly like you. You're it honey! My fondest dream!

I love you insanely,
Wayne

**Dear Wayne Albert,**

**What a winter we had. It was glorious at first. But when you went through the heart surgery, my heart stood still. I was more frightened than I've ever been in my life. It was like holding my breath, yet one complication after another seemed darker still.**

**It was a vivid way to experience the real truth. I don't want to live my life without you. I don't have to ever wonder: Do I love you with every fiber of my being? I do. You are more precious to me than words can describe. The rest of the time with Paul and Ann and the boys was loving, fulfilling, and fun!**

**I am more excited than ever since we have chosen our winter lifestyle!**

**I love you deeply,**

**Sidney**

Wayne kissed away my hurts.

June 24, 2006

Dear Sidney,

I know I looked pitiful in Roper hospital; but I knew for sure I'd recover because I was powerfully determined to overcome everything.

Your devoted presence gave me everything to live for. Living with you has been so wonderful that I wanted many more years with you. As many as I can get.

The heart surgery revealed so clearly what I live for and what I look forward to each day. I saw the hurt and fear in your face each day and I resolved to spend the rest of my life shielding you from your own hurt. To care for you in the most protective way. To be the delivery boy of joy and happiness for you. That's who I am and it's a little selfish too because that's how I get joy and happiness.

I love you powerfully,
Wayne.

My sweetheart Wayne,

This is such a blessed time even though it is stressful. I am falling more and more in love with you. It is as if my awareness has been awakened at a deeper level. I am discovering you all over again. This love is at a great depth. It is so exquisite it hurts in my heart and throat. I realize the treasure I have in you. I look forward to an even brighter future to know we can merge as one in spirit, love, and thought. We are the poem.

I love you deeply,
Sidney

My precious Sidney,

Your absence this past two weeks feels similar to when electric power goes out in our neighborhood. Nothing works right, every task is more difficult, and we just struggle to get by until the power is restored. I'm just struggling to get by until you return, and I can resume living again.

All my energies, my skills, my thoughts, my ambitions, my dreams and devotion are devoted to you. And to us becoming the most wonderful and beautiful couple that ever walked this earth. I'm saturated with you and it feels magnificent.

As God infused this physical world with his holy spirit, he infused us into each other. We have truly become one. And isn't that wonderful?

I know that is why I was given life on Earth, to find and merge with you Sidney. I feel absolutely safe with you. With no obstructions to a total connection with you. I'm struggling for better words to express the depth of my feelings for you but there are no adequate words. Sidney, the bottom line is this: we're a beautiful couple for eternity and that's a long time.

I love you as my perfect mate,

Wayne

"We could have spread our wings
and done a thousand things..."

Dear Wayne,

In the quiet of the night, I can feel so many wonderful and beautiful feelings for you. I love what you are: naturally helpful. You delight with simple things; you love music that is sweet from a more innocent time.

Like the song from my fair lady, "I could have danced all night and still have danced some more. I could have spread my wings and done a thousand things I've never done before."

I appreciate your loving devotion and feel more secure than I ever have in my entire life. You willingly work at us having a relationship like no other. I feel cherished by you, and I cherish you.

We can both search for the deeper meaning. Our love is a kind of fulfillment that is difficult to describe. I feel like our life has been very valuable and has made a difference in our world. To walk hand-in-hand with you trying to make this a better world is thrilling. You are a good, honest, high moral, gracious man of integrity. It is hard to believe I got all that I could possibly want in a man in you. My heart is yours Wayne.

I love you deeper than the ocean,

Sidney

**Dear Sidney,**

**Every morning when I wake up and see you, I feel peace. Confident we will have a beautiful day together! I know I am totally wanted by my genetic celebrity. You are the best of the best. You are unquestionably spiritual, moral, honest, gorgeous, and good to the bone. What a catch you are! God has blessed me beyond my wildest hopes!**

**With you, Sidney, I am completely contented and fulfilled! It doesn't get any better than this. When we're around family or friends, I'm so proud to be seen having you as my wife. You're my crowning jewel. I like to show you off. Like saying: "Look what I got! I'm so proud of you!"**

**Words fall short.**

**I love you without end,**

**Wayne**

**Dear Wayne,**

**We do have so many breathtaking moments, our whole life is a wondrous adventure. Imagine all we've done since the last entry in this book. With you I live a lifetime of memories with each adventure. I love you from the deepest part of my soul.**

**All my love,**
**Sidney**

I'm sorry you missed this 5-generation picture of those you loved.

November 7th, 2011

My dearest Sidney,

You've been to Lansing today and your absence overwhelms me with an awareness of how precious and meaningful you are to me. I am the one you can turn to every time and for any reason. You've taken my love and we are together forever. You have completed me. You are the one I was born to find, my incredible blessing.

Our hearts beat as one. We share one mind and one purpose. My attachment to you leaves me without the words to express. Such a love must last forever. You are my love, my fulfillment, my purpose. I gladly give my life to you and for you.

I am yours in love,

Wayne

You can count on me.

**October 15th, 2013,**

**Breast Cancer Challenge**

**My darling Wayne,**

**I am struggling with trying to express how I feel about you and it is very difficult. The words are not there to describe it. I love you for your dedication and love. I love you because of your deep commitment and your strong loyalty. I Love You because you genuinely care for me and my good. You are my hero.**

**You give totally of yourself. You have been through this awful cancer scare without complaint and you have sacrificed for me. I could not feel more cherished. If for no other reason I could not die and leave you alone. You are my companion through to eternity. You are the Heart of my Heart and Soul of my Soul.**

**I Love You dear Husband,**

**Sidney**

Committed and determined.

My dear Sidney,

You're coming home today. The moment I've dreamed of ever since you left to walk the El Camino trail. I'm incomplete without you and my only purpose is to rejoin you. You did it! You walked 550 miles on the same path as the Apostle James. You can't believe how proud I am of you. To wake up every morning knowing you must walk another 17 miles today. WHEW!!!

You define the words "commitment" and "determination," sweetheart. You've got what it takes and more. In your absence I got to know the true meaning of desperate loneliness. I don't want to ever live without you. Without you my life is meaningless, and with you it is fulfilling beyond measure.

Welcome home sweetheart. I love you madly,

Your Wayne

Dear Wayne,

It really touched me when you brought me the little cheese crackers on the little shell serving dish. Not only that, but your reason for doing so. You had dreamed something that strongly urged you to do a sweet act of love for me. I did feel loved and adored. After 35 years I still feel our fresh romance. I love the man and husband that you are. You love me for me. You have nurtured our marriage and made it first of all earthly things. I feel completely and spiritually connected to you. You are my love, my friend, and my companion.

I love you deeply,

Sidney

# LAST THOUGHTS AND CONSIDERATIONS

**FOR COUPLES WHO WANT TO ENHANCE THEIR RELATIONSHIP, THESE ARE MERELY SUGGESTIONS:**

**1) Be positive in your energy and actions to your mate.**
**2) NEVER, never criticize, it is toxic to relationships and tears down your mate's spirit.**
**3) Make it a habit to uplift your spouse. Never, never take them below zero.**
**4) Be a Good Finder not a Fault Finder.**
**5) Love what you see and see what you love.**
**6) Tell your mate one thing you love about them every day.**
**7) Discuss your relationship often and express your common dreams.**
**8) Tell your mate how they bless your life.**
**9) Be fearlessly vulnerable.**
**10) Offer your heart with open hands to each other.**

**11) Be loyal, truthful and act with integrity.**
**12) Never take anger to bed with you. Leave it outside to cool off.**
**13) Inspire your spouse. Shine your light upon them.**
**14) Offer your mate the gift of kindness.**
**15) Be best friends with each other.**
**16) Pray and worship together.**
**17) Be playmates.**
**18) Nurture humor and positivity.**

**19) When it is time to be serious, be SERIOUS. When it is time to laugh, LAUGH.**
**20) ENJOY THE JOURNEY AND DISPLAY THE JOY TO YOUR MATE.**

**-The Beginning-**

Two souls merged and we were one.

www.ingramcontent.com/pod-product-compliance
Lightning Source LLC
LaVergne TN
LVHW010612110826
845149LV00003B/881